# 15 Minutes Recipes for Two

# 50 Healthy Two-Serving 15 Minutes Recipes

Louise Davidson

**Copyrights**

All rights reserved © 2018 by Louise Davidson and The Cookbook Publisher. No part of this publication or the information in it may be quoted from or reproduced in any form by means such as printing, scanning, photocopying, or otherwise without prior written permission of the copyright holder.

**Disclaimer and Terms of Use**

Effort has been made to ensure that the information in this book is accurate and complete. However, the author and the publisher do not warrant the accuracy of the information, text, and graphics contained within the book due to the rapidly changing nature of science, research, known and unknown facts, and internet. The author and the publisher do not hold any responsibility for errors, omissions, or contrary interpretation of the subject matter herein. This book is presented solely for motivational and informational purposes only.

**ISBN: 978-1720473817**

**Printed in the United States**

# Contents

Introduction _____ 1

Breakfast Recipes _____ 3

Chicken & Poultry Recipes _____ 9

Beef Recipes _____ 17

Fish & Seafood Recipes _____ 25

Pork & Lamb Recipes _____ 33

Vegetarian/Vegan Recipes _____ 43

Desserts _____ 53

Recipe Index _____ 59

Also by Louise Davidson _____ 61

Appendix Cooking Conversion Charts _____ 63

# Introduction

Whether you are a homemaker or part of a working couple, time has become a very precious asset. Our routines are filled with hundreds of tasks, both big and small. There never seems to be enough time to finish them, and so there is increasing interest in healthy meals that can be prepared quickly.

We want to enjoy delicious, wholesome meals at the table to nourish ourselves and spend a few minutes with our loved ones after a tiring day. When you only have to prepare meals for two, there are ways to save a lot of preparation and cooking time. If you are struggling to find adequate time to make wholesome meals every day, then how about learning recipes that take only 15 minutes to prepare?

When we're so busy, it's more important than ever to eat nutritious meals. We need energy from quality nutrients, and we also need to fight off viruses and infections that might prey upon our overworked bodies. This book includes nutritious recipes to prepare in 15 minutes for breakfast, lunch, dinner, or dessert. Explore our dedicated chapters on breakfast, chicken & poultry, beef, pork & lamb, vegetarian/vegan and dessert!

This book focuses on quick cooking and delivering a practical solution to people who always find themselves running short of time to cook wholesome, delicious meals. With just 15 minutes of preparation time, the two of you can effortlessly prepare and enjoy healthy meals every day.

**Quick Cooking Tips**

- Plan your meals ahead and prepare by peeling, trimming, chopping, and slicing the required veggies and fruits in advance. Store them in containers in the refrigerator until ready to use. You can take them out and let them sit at room temperature for a few minutes before using them for recipes.

- Keep track of staples on your shelves such as cooking oil, basic spices, seasonings, etc. Make a list and purchase these things when you're running low. This saves you extra trips to the store, and also having to change your meal plan because something is missing.

- Make a meal plan in advance and if possible, make note of the recipes you want to prepare in a diary or notebook for a whole week, or even a month. This way, you can shop for sales, or buy in bulk.

- Starches like rice and mashed potato keep well in the fridge for up to a week, so make leftovers! You can reheat in seconds what would otherwise take half an hour to cook. Change the flavors up by adding spices or different sauces.

Get ready to explore the secrets of preparing healthy, quick meals. Let's get started!

# Breakfast Recipes

## Spiced Orange Couscous

*Serves: 2 - Prep. time: 2–3 minutes - Cooking time: 10 minutes*

**Ingredients:**
½ teaspoon ground cinnamon
⅛ teaspoon ground cloves
1 ½ cups orange juice
¾ cups dry couscous
¼ cup dried fruit of your choice
¼ cup chopped almonds or walnuts

**Preparation:**
1. In a small saucepan, bring the orange juice to a boil.
2. Add the cinnamon, cloves, and couscous, and remove the pot from the heat.
3. Cover, and allow it to sit until the couscous softens, about 4–5 minutes.
4. Fluff the couscous; mix in the dried fruit and nuts. Serve immediately.

**Nutrition facts per serving**
Calories 269, fat 6.2 g, carbs 44 g,
Protein 6 g, sodium 29 mg

# Cinnamon Apple Classic Oatmeal

*Serves: 2 - Prep. time: 5 minutes - Cooking time: 10 minutes*

### Ingredients:
1 ¼ cups apple cider
1 apple, peeled, cored, and chopped
⅔ cup rolled oats
1 teaspoon cinnamon, ground
1 tablespoon maple syrup

### Preparation:
1. In a medium saucepan, bring the apple cider to a boil over medium-high heat. Gradually stir in the apple, oats, and cinnamon.
2. Bring the mixture to a boil, and turn down the heat to low. Simmer until the oatmeal thickens, 3–4 minutes.
3. Mix in the maple syrup. Serve hot.

### Nutrition facts per serving
Calories 278, fat 2.3 g, carbs 26.5 g,
Protein 4.6 g, sodium 42 mg

# Flax Almond Crepes

*Serves: 2 - Prep. time: 2–3 minutes - Cooking time: 12 minutes*

**Ingredients:**
2 eggs
3 egg whites
¼ cup almond milk, unsweetened
¼ cup coconut flour
2 tablespoons ground flaxseed
½ teaspoon baking soda
Cream and/or strawberries to serve

**Preparation:**
1. In a food processor, blend all the ingredients EXCEPT the cream and strawberries until smooth.
2. Heat a large skillet over medium.
3. Spoon some batter into the skillet and swirl to make a large, thin crepe.
4. Cook for 2–3 minutes, until the crepe is set and light golden on the bottom.
5. Flip and cook for 1–2 more minutes.
6. Repeat with leftover batter.
7. Enjoy with chopped strawberries, and/or cream.

**Nutrition facts per serving**
Calories 248, fat 10.4 g, carbs 13.1 g,
Protein 15 g, sodium 652 mg

# Berry Breakfast Granola

*Serves: 2 - Prep. time: 5 minutes - Cooking time: 0 minutes*

**Ingredients:**
1 cup granola
½ cup walnuts
1 (14 ounce) can coconut milk, refrigerated overnight
1 cup mixed berries of your choice (strawberries, blueberries, raspberries, etc.)

**Preparation:**
1. In two breakfast bowls, layer the coconut milk, granola, walnuts, and berries.
2. Gently stir and serve immediately.

**Nutrition facts per serving**
Calories 452, fat 32 g, carbs 31.8 g,
Protein 11.7 g, sodium 47 mg

# Nutty Peach Breakfast Bowl

*Serves: 2 - Prep. time: 8–10 minutes - Cooking time: 0 minutes*

**Ingredients:**
1 ripe peach, pitted and thinly sliced
1 tablespoon mint, chopped
½ cup low-fat cottage cheese
¼ cup walnuts, chopped
1 teaspoon honey
Zest of 1 lemon

**Preparation:**
1. In a dry skillet, toast the walnuts for a few minutes until they are aromatic.
2. Spoon the cottage cheese into your bowls, and top with the peach slices and walnuts.
3. Mix in the honey, zest, and mint.
4. Serve fresh.

**Nutrition facts per serving**
Calories 175, fat 11 g, carbs 12.3 g,
Protein 10 g, sodium 234 mg

# Chicken & Poultry Recipes

## Spiced Pepper Turkey

*Serves: 2 - Prep. time: 5 minutes - Cooking time: 8–10 minutes*

**Ingredients:**
6 (2 ounce) turkey breast cutlets
¼ teaspoon garlic powder
¼ teaspoon salt
¼ teaspoon black pepper
2 teaspoons olive oil
1 large red bell pepper, cut in rings
¼ cup balsamic vinegar

**Preparation:**
1. Sprinkle the turkey cutlets with garlic powder, salt, and black pepper.
2. Heat the olive oil in a nonstick skillet over medium-high heat.
3. Add the turkey pieces and cook for 2–3 minutes on each side, until they are cooked through and lightly brown.
4. Transfer the cutlets to a serving platter.
5. Add the red bell pepper to the skillet, and sauté for 3 minutes, stirring occasionally.
6. Spoon the peppers on top of the turkey cutlets.
7. Add the balsamic vinegar to the skillet and cook for 1 minute.
8. Spoon over the turkey, and serve.

**Nutrition facts per serving**
Calories 276, fat 5.5 g, carbs 10.7 g,
Protein 43 g, sodium 457 mg

# Barbecue Orange Chicken

*Serves: 2 - Prep. time: 2–3 minutes, plus marinating time – Cooking time: 12 minutes*

**Ingredients:**
1 tablespoon jalapeño peppers, seeded and minced
½ teaspoon allspice
2 tablespoons red onion, chopped
1 tablespoon soy sauce
1 tablespoon fresh thyme
¼ cup chopped green onions
1 teaspoon fresh ginger, peeled and minced
1 clove garlic, crushed and minced
1 tablespoon olive oil
2 tablespoons orange juice
Salt and pepper to taste
2 bone-in chicken breasts, skin on
Lime wedges for serving

**Preparation:**
1. In a food processor, combine all the ingredients EXCEPT the chicken and the lime wedges.
2. Purée until smooth. Place the chicken pieces in a resealable bag, and pour in the marinade.
3. Shake well and put it in the refrigerator for 4–8 hours.
4. Preheat your grill to medium-high.
5. Drain any excess marinade, and put the chicken on the grill.
6. Grill on each side for 5–6 minutes, until browned and cooked through.
7. Serve, and enjoy.

**Nutrition facts per serving**
Calories 232, fat 12.8 g, carbs 6.2 g,
Protein 25.6 g, sodium 587 mg

# Chicken Lettuce Cups

*Serves: 2 - Prep. time: 5 minutes - Cooking time: 4 minutes*

## Ingredients:
1 ½ tablespoons vegetable oil
12 ounces chicken breast, ground
1 clove garlic, minced
2 shallots, diced
¼ red onion, diced
Chopped chilies, to taste
1 head iceberg lettuce, leaves separated
1 teaspoon soy sauce, low-sodium
Juice of half a lime
1 tablespoon fish sauce
Handful of cilantro

## Preparation:
1. Heat the oil in a medium saucepan and add the chicken.
2. Break the meat into smaller pieces and cook for 2–3 minutes, until it is evenly browned.
3. Add the garlic, shallots, red onion, and chilies.
4. Cook the mixture for 1–2 minutes, until the vegetables begin to soften.
5. Add the lime juice, fish sauce, and soy sauce. Mix well.
6. Arrange the lettuce leaves on serving plates, and spoon the mix evenly over them; serve warm!

## Nutrition facts per serving
Calories 203, fat 13.5 g, carbs 7.4 g,
Protein 17 g, sodium 856 mg

# Lemongrass Pasta Chicken

*Serves: 2 - Prep. time: 3–5 minutes - Cooking time: 13 minutes*

**Ingredients:**
1 teaspoon olive oil
½ pound boneless skinless chicken breast, cubed
2 cloves garlic, crushed and minced
½ tablespoon ginger, grated
½ tablespoon fresh lemongrass, chopped
¼ cup soy sauce
½ tablespoon chili garlic paste
¼ cup creamy natural peanut butter
½ tablespoon lime juice
1 teaspoon sesame oil
1 cup chicken stock
½ pound angel hair pasta
¼ cup peanuts, chopped

**Preparation:**
1. In a cast iron skillet, heat the olive oil over medium.
2. Add the chicken and sauté until browned, 4–5 minutes.
3. Add the garlic, ginger, lemongrass, soy sauce, and chili garlic paste. Combine well.
4. Add the peanut butter, lime juice, sesame oil, and chicken stock.
5. Increase the heat and bring the mixture to a boil.
6. Add the pasta and reduce the heat to simmer.
7. Cook 5–7 minutes, or until the pasta is tender.
8. Remove from heat and add the peanuts; serve warm.

**Nutrition facts per serving**
Calories 542, fat 27.2 g, carbs 45.6 g,
Protein 38.8 g, sodium 1356 mg

# Spiced Turkey Burger Patties

*Makes 4 patties - Prep. time: 2–3 minutes – Cooking time: 10 minutes*

### Ingredients:
1 pound ground turkey
Salt and pepper to taste
½ tablespoon jalapeño pepper
Zest and juice of half a lime
1 shallot, peeled and minced
2 tablespoons cilantro, chopped
1 teaspoon cumin
1 teaspoon paprika
Cooking spray
For serving: buns, cheese, vegetables

### Preparation:
1. Combine all the ingredients in a bowl, and form four burger patties.
2. Heat a large, non-stick skillet over medium, and coat it with cooking spray.
3. Arrange the patties in the skillet and cook for 5 minutes on each side.
4. Make burgers with your choice of buns, cheese, and veggies.

### Nutrition facts per serving
Calories 378, fat 18.6 g, carbs 16.4 g,
Protein 48 g, sodium 624 mg

# Fried Asparagus Chicken

*Serves: 2 - Prep. time: 2–3 minutes - Cooking time: 8 minutes*

**Ingredients:**

1 tablespoon olive oil
1 cup chicken thigh fillets, cut in strips
2 cloves garlic, minced
3–5 ounces asparagus spears, trimmed and cut in 3-inch strips
1 tablespoon lemon juice
Salt and pepper to taste
¼ cup chicken broth

**Preparation:**

1. Heat the olive oil in a skillet or wok over high heat. Add the chicken, garlic, asparagus, lemon juice, salt, and pepper.
2. Cook for 4–5 minutes, stirring occasionally.
3. Turn down the heat and mix in the broth.
4. Simmer for 3–4 minutes. Serve warm.

**Nutrition facts per serving**

Calories 163, fat 9 g, carbs 2.6 g,
Protein 12.6 g, sodium 53 mg

# Classic Honey Chicken

*Serves: 2 - Prep. time: 2–3 minutes - Cooking time: 7–8 minutes*

**Ingredients:**
1 tablespoon olive oil
6 ounces boneless chicken, cut in strips
Salt and pepper to taste
2 tablespoons fresh basil, chopped
2 tablespoons honey
1 tablespoon balsamic vinegar
For serving: 1 cup chopped veggies

**Preparation:**
1. Heat the oil in a skillet over medium-high heat.
2. Sprinkle the chicken with salt and pepper.
3. Cook for 4–5 minutes, or until the juices run clear.
4. Add the rest of the ingredients and cook for 2–3 minutes.
5. Serve with chopped veggies.

**Nutrition facts per serving**
Calories 172, fat 7 g, carbs 5.1 g,
Protein 22 g, sodium 564 mg

# Mayo Grilled Chicken

*Serves: 2 - Prep. time: 2 minutes - Cooking time: 14–15 minutes*

**Ingredients:**
2 tablespoons mayonnaise
1 teaspoon steak sauce
2 teaspoons Dijon mustard
2 tablespoons honey
4 boneless, skinless chicken breast halves
Cooking spray

**Preparation:**
1. Preheat a grill or barbecue to medium-high heat.
2. Mix the mayonnaise, steak sauce, mustard, and honey in a mixing bowl.
3. Set aside half the sauce, and brush the rest over the chicken.
4. Coat the grate with cooking spray, and arrange the chicken on it. Grill for 7–8 minutes on each side, or until the meat is no longer pink.
5. Brush the chicken with more sauce as you cook it, and serve warm.

**Nutrition facts per serving**
Calories 442, fat 18 g, carbs 16.7 g,
Protein 47.2 g, sodium 513 mg

# Beef Recipes

## Bacon Veggie Steak

*Serves: 2 - Prep. time: 2–3 minutes - Cooking time: 14 minutes*

### Ingredients:
2 slices bacon
1 (6 ounce) beef tenderloin steak (about 1 ¼ inches thick), trimmed
Salt and pepper to taste
3 cups romaine lettuce, torn
½ cup grape tomatoes, halved
¼ cup salad dressing of your choice (optional)

### Preparation:
1. In a skillet, fry the bacon for 2–3 minutes, until crispy. Remove it from the pan and let it cool. Chop or crumble it, and set it aside.
2. Sprinkle the steak evenly with salt and pepper, and cook it in the bacon drippings for 3–4 minutes on each side, or until it reaches the desired state of doneness.
3. Remove the steak to a cutting board, and let it sit for 2–3 minutes before slicing it thinly.
4. Meanwhile, toss the lettuce and tomato with the dressing in a mixing bowl.
5. Divide the salad among two serving plates, and top with steak slices and bacon.

### Nutrition facts per serving
Calories 233, fat 14.2 g, carbs 8 g,
Protein 20.3 g, sodium 754 mg

# Barbecued Mirin Short Ribs

*Serves: 2 - Prep. time: 4–5 min (plus overnight marinating time)
Cooking time: 10 minutes*

### Ingredients:
2 tablespoons mirin
4 tablespoon dark brown sugar
¼ cup soy sauce
2 tablespoons rice vinegar
2 teaspoons sesame oil
1 clove garlic, minced
1 small green onion, chopped
1 pound short ribs

### Preparation:
1. In a mixing bowl, combine the mirin, brown sugar, soy sauce, rice vinegar, sesame oil, garlic, and green onion.
2. Pour it into a resealable plastic bag.
3. Add the short ribs and seal the bag. Shake well and refrigerate overnight.
4. Preheat the grill to medium-high heat.
5. Remove the ribs from the marinade, and discard the marinade. Grill for 4-5 minutes on each side.

### Nutrition facts per serving
Calories 584, fat 33 g, carbs 24.3 g,
Protein 21.1 g, sodium 1423 mg

# Garlic Steak with Greens

*Serves: 2 - Prep. time: 2–3 minutes - Cooking time: 10 minutes*

**Ingredients:**
2 tablespoons butter
1 clove garlic, minced
½ teaspoon garlic powder
1 pound sirloin steak, beef tip
Salt and pepper to taste
For serving: salad greens, chopped
Cooking spray

**Preparation:**
1. Preheat your grill and coat the grates with cooking spray.
2. In a medium saucepan, melt the butter over low heat.
3. Add the garlic and garlic powder. Stir and set aside.
4. Sprinkle salt and pepper over the steak.
5. Grill for 4–5 minutes per side, occasionally brushing the steak with garlic butter.
6. Serve with fresh greens on the side.

**Nutrition facts per serving**
Calories 541, fat 28 g, carbs 36.2 g,
Protein 37.2 g, sodium 1217 mg

# Broccoli Garlic Steak

*Serves: 2 - Prep. time: 2–3 minutes - Cooking time: 10 minutes*

**Ingredients:**
1 tablespoon vegetable oil
8 ounces beef steak, cut in thin strips
1 tablespoon brown sugar
½ tablespoon honey
½ tablespoon sesame seeds
2 tablespoons soy sauce
1 teaspoon sesame oil
1 teaspoon garlic paste
1 clove garlic, crushed and minced
½ cup yellow onion, sliced
½ cup savoy cabbage, shredded
1 cup broccoli florets
½ cup carrots, thinly sliced

**Preparation:**
1. Heat a skillet over medium, and add the vegetable oil.
2. Add the steak and sauté for 2–3 minutes, or until browned. Set it aside.
3. Add the brown sugar, honey, sesame seeds, soy sauce, sesame oil, and garlic paste.
4. Stir until fragrant, about 1 minute.
5. Add the garlic and onion. Sauté for 2 minutes.
6. Add the savoy cabbage, broccoli, and carrots. Cook for 3 minutes.
7. Mix in the meat and its juices, and serve warm.

**Nutrition facts per serving**
Calories 498, fat 24 g, carbs 17.2 g,
Protein 28.6 g, sodium 1014 mg

# Jalapeño Sweet Beef

*Serves: 2 - Prep. time: 5 minutes - Cooking time: 10 minutes*

**Ingredients:**
1 pound flank steak, cut in thin strips
2 tablespoons cornstarch
1 tablespoon canola oil
1 jalapeño pepper, seeded and diced
1 (1 inch) piece of ginger, peeled and diced
5 cloves garlic, minced
5 scallions, thinly sliced

For the Sauce:
½ cup brown sugar
½ cup soy sauce
2 teaspoons cornstarch

**Preparation:**
1. Combine the beef and cornstarch in a bowl. Set it aside.
2. Place a small saucepan over medium heat, and add all the sauce ingredients. Stir well, and bring it to a boil.
3. Set the sauce aside to cool down.
4. Meanwhile, heat a large skillet over high heat.
5. Add the canola oil, jalapeño pepper, and ginger. Cook for 4–5 minutes to soften the pepper.
6. Add the garlic and coated beef; cook for 1 minute on each side.
7. Pour in the sauce, and stir until well coated. Allow to simmer for 1 minute.
8. Remove the skillet from the heat, and top with the scallions. Serve.

**Nutrition facts per serving**
Calories 604, fat 17 g, carbs 41.1 g,
Protein 33 g, sodium 98 mg

# Bean Sprout Beef Salad

*Serves: 2 - Prep. time: 5 minutes - Cooking time: 10 minutes*

**Ingredients:**
2 teaspoons vegetable oil
½ pound rump steak
2 tablespoons sweet chili sauce
½ tablespoon fish sauce
½ tablespoon lime juice
1 clove garlic, crushed
1 tablespoon mint leaves, chopped
1 cucumber, chopped
3 large tomatoes, quartered
1 cup bean sprouts
1 tablespoons cilantro, chopped

**Preparation:**
1. In a saucepan; heat the oil and cook the beef until it is browned evenly, 8–10 minutes.
2. Remove it from the heat and slice it thinly.
3. In a mixing bowl, combine the sweet chili sauce, fish sauce, and lime juice. Add the garlic and mint leaves; combine well.
4. Mix the cucumber, tomato, and sprouts in a mixing bowl.
5. Add the beef and sauce, and mix well. Top with cilantro.
6. Serve, and enjoy.

**Nutrition facts per serving**
Calories 217, fat 8.5 g, carbs 9.3 g,
Protein 27.8 g, sodium 543 mg

# Beef Burger Patties

*Makes 4 patties - Prep. time: 5 minutes –
Cooking time: 3 minutes*

## *Ingredients:*
1 egg
¼ cup breadcrumbs
½ onion, finely chopped
2 teaspoons mustard
½ teaspoon thyme
½ teaspoon paprika
1 pound lean ground beef
½ cup grated cheese
Salt and pepper to taste
Cooking spray
For serving: buns, cheese and vegetables

## *Preparation:*
1. Beat the egg in a bowl. Add the breadcrumbs, onion, mustard, thyme, and paprika.
2. Combine well and add the beef, salt, and pepper.
3. Add the cheese and combine well.
4. Prepare 4 patties from the mixture.
5. Preheat the grill to medium, and coat it with cooking spray.
6. Arrange the patties on the grill, and cook for 5–6 minutes per side.
7. Make burgers with your choice of buns, cheese, and veggies.

## *Nutrition facts per serving*
Calories 624, fat 36 g, carbs 3.6 g,
Protein 58.3 g, sodium 483 mg

# Berry Sauce Beef

*Serves: 2 - Prep. time: 2–3 minutes - Cooking time: 13 minutes*

**Ingredients:**
1 tablespoon olive oil
1 sprig thyme
2 (6 ounce) beef steaks
Salt and pepper to taste
4 small onions, sliced
¼ cup red wine
1 teaspoon honey
½ cup mixed berries

**Preparation:**
1. In a skillet, heat the olive oil over medium and add the thyme.
2. Add the beef and onions, cook for 3-4 minutes on each side and season with salt and pepper.
3. Remove the steaks and set them aside.
4. Add the red wine and honey to the pan. Mix well.
5. Add the berries and cook for 4–5 minutes, stirring occasionally. Remove the thyme twig.
6. Place the steaks on serving plates; top with the berry sauce, and serve.

**Nutrition facts per serving**
Calories 174, fat 12 g, carbs 8.1 g,
Protein 5.2 g, sodium 38 mg

# Fish & Seafood Recipes

## Sardine Arugula Salad

*Serves: 2 - Prep. time: 5–8 minutes - Cooking time: 0 minutes*

**Ingredients:**
1 pack of 2 whole sardine fillets in olive oil, drained
Juice of half a lemon
¼ cup olive oil
Salt and pepper to taste
½ teaspoon Dijon mustard
2 diced tomatoes
1 small cucumber, peeled and diced
½ bunch flat-leaf parsley, chopped
1 cup arugula, trimmed and chopped
½ red onion, thinly sliced

**Preparation:**
1. Drain and chop the sardine fillets and set them aside.
2. Whisk together the lemon juice, olive oil, salt, pepper, and mustard in a mixing bowl. Set it aside.
3. In a salad bowl, mix the vegetables with the parsley. Combine well.
4. Arrange the fillets on top of the salad mixture.
5. Drizzle the mustard dressing over the salad; toss well, and serve.

**Nutrition facts per serving**
Calories 268, fat 22.3 g, carbs 6.2 g,
Protein 3 g, sodium 19 mg

# Tuna Pineapple Treat

*Serves: 2 - Prep. time: 8–10 minutes - Cooking time: 0 minutes*

**Ingredients:**
2 tablespoons mayonnaise
1 teaspoon lemon juice
Pinch smoked paprika
Salt and pepper to taste
1 large can white tuna in oil, drained
1 tablespoon green olives, chopped
4 pineapple slices

**Preparation:**
1. In a bowl, combine the mayonnaise, lemon juice, paprika, salt, and pepper.
2. Stir in the tuna and olives. Combine well.
3. Arrange two pineapple slices on plates, and top each with half the tuna mixture.
4. Arrange the remaining two pineapple slices on top, and serve as a sandwich.

**Nutrition facts per serving**
Calories 317, fat 18 g, carbs 16.3 g,
Protein 23.1 g, sodium 483 mg

# Shrimp Potato Salad

*Serves: 2 - Prep. time: 5 minutes - Cooking time: 3 minutes*

## Ingredients:
5 ounces boiled shrimp, peeled and deveined, tails intact
½ fennel bulb, thinly sliced
1 medium potato, boiled and thinly sliced
½ white onion, thinly sliced
¼ cup green olives
3 cups lettuce, torn

Dressing:
1 tablespoon Dijon mustard
¼ cup olive oil
1 tablespoon balsamic vinegar
⅛ teaspoon dried thyme
Salt and pepper to taste

## Preparation:
1. Prepare the dressing: Combine the mustard, olive oil, balsamic vinegar, and thyme in a bowl. Season with pepper and salt. Set it aside.
2. Combine the shrimp, fennel, boiled potato, white onion, green olives, and lettuce in a mixing bowl. Toss to thoroughly mix.
3. Place the salad on serving plates and top with the vinaigrette.

## Nutrition facts per serving
Calories 411, fat 23.2 g, carbs 19 g,
Protein 34.8 g, sodium 853 mg

# Whitefish and Veggies

*Serves: 2 - Prep. time: 2–3 minutes - Cooking time: 6 minutes*

**Ingredients:**
1 tablespoon vegetable oil
2 (5 ounce) whitefish fillets
½ tablespoon all-purpose flour
1 green onion, sliced
½ cucumber, sliced into sticks
1 tablespoon walnuts, chopped
½ cup cilantro
¼ cup your choice of salad dressing
Lime wedges to serve

**Preparation:**
1. Place a frying pan over medium heat, and warm the oil.
2. Coat the fish fillets with flour. Fry them in the vegetable oil for 2–3 minutes on each side. Remove them from the heat and set them aside.
3. In a mixing bowl, combine the green onion, cucumber, walnuts, cilantro, and dressing.
4. Divide the salad between 2 dinner plates, and arrange a piece of fish on top. Serve with lime wedges.

**Nutrition facts per serving**
Calories 197, fat 14 g, carbs 3.3 g,
Protein 16.8 g, sodium 26 mg

# Tuna Lettuce Pasta Time

*Serves: 2 - Prep. time: 2–3 minutes - Cooking time: 10 minutes*

## Ingredients:
1 ½ cups fusilli pasta, cooked
½ cup canned tuna flakes, drained
1 medium ripe tomato, diced
2 black olives, sliced
2 green olives, sliced
2 cups romaine lettuce

Vinaigrette:
¼ cup olive oil
1 ½ tablespoons red wine vinegar
½ tablespoon Dijon mustard
½ teaspoon dill weed, finely chopped
Salt and pepper to taste

## Preparation:
1. Prepare the dressing: Mix the olive oil, red wine vinegar, mustard, and dill in a bowl. Season with pepper and salt.
2. Mix the pasta with the tuna, tomato, and olives in a large bowl.
3. Drizzle with the prepared vinaigrette and toss well.
4. Arrange the lettuce on serving plates, and serve the salad over it.

## Nutrition facts per serving
Calories 605, fat 24 g, carbs 31.2 g,
Protein 24 g, sodium 38 mg

# Wine and Tomato Mussels

*Serves: 2 - Prep. time: 2–3 minutes - Cooking time: 7 minutes*

**Ingredients:**
1 tablespoon olive oil
1 small red onion, sliced
1 clove garlic, minced
½ teaspoon ginger, grated
1 cup red wine
1 cup stewed tomatoes
1 cup water
2 pounds mussels, cleaned, rinsed, and debearded
¼ cup cilantro, chopped
Salt and pepper to taste

**Preparation:**
1. Heat the oil in a large saucepan on medium-high heat.
2. Add the onion, garlic, and ginger, and cook until aromatic.
3. Add the wine, tomatoes, and water. Season with salt and pepper.
4. Bring the mixture to a boil, and add the mussels.
5. Cover, and cook the mussels for 5–7 minutes, until the shells open. Discard any mussels that do not open up.
6. Sprinkle with chopped cilantro, and serve.

**Nutrition facts per serving**
Calories 307, fat 9 g, carbs 21.8 g,
Protein 11 g, sodium 624 mg

# Buttery White Wine Prawns

*Serves: 2 - Prep. time: 5 minutes - Cooking time: 7 minutes*

**Ingredients:**
¼ cup butter
2 garlic cloves, minced
1 pound large prawns
2 tablespoons dry white wine
½ teaspoon sugar
2 tablespoons parsley leaves, chopped
2 tablespoons lemon juice
1 teaspoon fresh dill weed, chopped
Salt and pepper to taste

**Preparation:**
1. Melt the butter in a skillet over medium-high heat.
2. Add the garlic and cook until it releases its scent.
3. Add the prawns, wine, sugar, parsley, lemon juice, and dill.
4. Cook for 3-4 minutes, stirring frequently.
5. Season with salt and pepper, and serve warm.

**Nutrition facts per serving**
Calories 483, fat 23.5 g, carbs 5.3 g,
Protein 48 g, sodium 963 mg

# Pork & Lamb Recipes

## Grilled Pork Mango Meal

*Serves: 2 - Prep. time: 5 minutes - Cooking time: 10 minutes*

### Ingredients:
2 (4 ounce) pork loin chops, center cut, boneless
Salt and pepper to taste
1 teaspoon ground cumin
Cooking spray
1 (12 ounce) jar sliced mango, drained
½ cup rinsed and drained canned black beans
¼ cup salsa of your choice
1 tablespoon chopped cilantro

### Preparation:
1. Preheat your grill, and coat the grates with cooking spray.
2. Sprinkle both sides of the pork with salt, pepper, and cumin.
3. Coat the pork with cooking spray.
4. Place the chops on the grill, and cook for 5–6 minutes on each side.
5. While the pork grills, mix the mango, beans, and salsa in a mixing bowl.
6. Arrange the chops on a serving platter.
7. Spoon the salsa over the chops, and top with the cilantro.

### Nutrition facts per serving
Calories 278, fat 7 g, carbs 22.5 g,
Protein 27 g, sodium 508 mg

# Ham and Bacon Melt

*Serves: 2 - Prep. time: 2–3 minutes - Cooking time: 10 minutes*

**Ingredients:**
2 slices rye bread
6 thin slices deli ham
4 slices bacon, precooked
4 teaspoons Dijon mustard
2 thick slices tomato
2 slices Swiss cheese

**Preparation:**
1. Preheat your broiler.
2. Lay out the bread slices and spread 2 teaspoons of mustard on each slice.
3. Place the ham on the bread; top each with 2 pieces of bacon, a slice of tomato, and a slice of cheese.
4. Place the sandwiches on a baking sheet and broil them for 2 minutes. Serve warm.

**Nutrition facts per serving**
Calories 269, fat 11.2 g, carbs 17 g,
Protein 18.2 g, sodium 856 mg

# Spiced Lamb Sausages

*Serves: 2 - Prep. time: 5 minutes, plus marinating time – Cooking time: 10–12 minutes*

### Ingredients:
1 teaspoon ground cumin
1 teaspoon ground coriander
1 pound lean lamb, ground
½ tablespoon ginger paste
½ tablespoon green chili paste
¼ cup cilantro, chopped
1 teaspoon paprika
½ teaspoon cayenne pepper
1 onion, finely diced
¼ cup mint leaves, finely chopped
1 teaspoon salt
2 tablespoons vegetable oil

### Preparation:
1. In a bowl, combine all the ingredients EXCEPT the vegetable oil and mix well.
2. Cover the bowl with plastic, and marinate for at least 1–2 hours at room temperature.
3. Preheat a grill and oil the grate.
4. Shape the meat mixture into two sausage shapes and pierce them with skewers.
5. Grill for 10–12 minutes, turning them every 3 minutes.
6. Serve warm!

### Nutrition facts per serving
Calories 382, fat 19 g, carbs 2.8 g,
Protein 44.7 g, sodium 1156 mg

# Sweet Tarragon Lamb

*Serves: 2 - Prep. time: 5 minutes, plus marinating time – Cooking time: 5 minutes*

## Ingredients:
1 teaspoon garlic powder
1 teaspoon ground black pepper
¼ cup brown sugar
½ teaspoon salt
1 teaspoon cinnamon, ground
2 teaspoons ginger, ground
2 teaspoons dried tarragon
4 lamb chops
Cooking spray as needed

## Preparation:
1. In a bowl, thoroughly mix the garlic powder, black pepper, brown sugar, salt, cinnamon, ginger, and tarragon.
2. Coat the pieces of lamb with the ginger mix.
3. Cover the bowl with plastic and put in the fridge for 2 hours.
4. Preheat your grill and coat the grate using some cooking spray.
5. Cook the marinated lamb on the grill for 4–5 minutes, or until it is cooked through.
6. Serve warm.

## Nutrition facts per serving
Calories 581, fat 6.2 g, carbs 38.4 g,
Protein 31 g, sodium 384 mg

# Spiced Pita Lamb Burgers

*Serves: 2 - Prep. time: 2–3 minutes - Cooking time: 12 minutes*

**Ingredients:**
½ pound ground lamb
½ teaspoon white wine vinegar
½ teaspoon ground cumin
1 clove garlic, minced
1 tablespoon brown sugar
Salt and pepper to taste
1 tablespoon cilantro, finely chopped
1 tablespoon oregano, finely chopped
1 tablespoon mint leaves, finely chopped
⅛ teaspoon allspice, ground
¼ teaspoon red pepper flakes
2 pita bread rounds
2 ounces feta cheese, crumbled

**Preparation:**
1. In a bowl, combine the lamb with the vinegar, cumin, garlic, brown sugar, salt and pepper, cilantro, oregano, mint, allspice, and red pepper flakes.
2. Combine well, and form 2 burger patties.
3. Preheat your grill.
4. Cook the burgers on the grill for 5–6 minutes per side.
5. Toast the pita rounds for 20–30 seconds.
6. Place the burger patties in the pitas, and add the feta.
7. Serve warm.

**Nutrition facts per serving**
Calories 484, fat 28 g, carbs 24.6 g,
Protein 32.1 g, sodium 452 mg

# Peas and Lemongrass Pork

*Serves: 2 - Prep. time: 2–3 minutes - Cooking time: 10 minutes*

**Ingredients:**
½ tablespoon olive oil
1 clove garlic, crushed and minced
½ cup carrots, diced
¼ cup celery, diced
½ pound ground pork
1 cup fresh sweet peas
1 teaspoon ginger, grated
1 teaspoon lemongrass, chopped
1 tablespoon soy sauce
½ tablespoon oyster sauce
½ tablespoon rice vinegar
½ teaspoon salt
½ teaspoon black pepper

**Preparation:**
1. In a skillet and heat the oil over medium.
2. Add the garlic, carrots, and celery. Cook for 3–4 minutes, stirring occasionally.
3. Add the pork and continue cooking until it is browned, 4–5 minutes.
4. Add the peas and season with ginger, lemongrass, soy sauce, oyster sauce, and rice vinegar.
5. Combine well and season with salt and pepper. Cook for 2 more minutes and serve warm.

**Nutrition facts per serving**
Calories 428, fat 18.6 g, carbs 31.2 g,
Protein 16 g, sodium 1874 mg

# Mushroom Basil Pork Fry

*Serves: 2 - Prep. time: 2–3 minutes, plus marinating time – Cooking time: 8–10 minutes*

**Ingredients:**
1 teaspoon olive oil
½ pound pork loin, cubed
1 cup mushrooms, sliced
¼ cup carrot, sliced
¼ cup zucchini, sliced
½ cup basil leaves
For serving: chopped greens
Steamed rice (optional)

Marinade:
3 tablespoons fish sauce
1 clove garlic, diced
¼ cup red wine
2 teaspoons sesame oil
1 teaspoon grated ginger
¼ cup scallions, chopped
½ teaspoon black pepper

**Preparation:**
1. Make the marinade by combining all the ingredients in a bowl.
2. Place the marinade and meat in a resealable bag. Shake well and marinade for 1–2 hours.
3. In a skillet, heat the olive oil over medium.
4. Cook the marinated pork for 3–5 minutes, reserving the marinade.

5. Add the mushrooms, carrot, zucchini, and basil; stir fry for 2 minutes.
6. Add the marinade liquid, bring it to a boil, and cook for 1 minute.
7. Serve with chopped greens or steamed rice.

***Nutrition facts per serving***
Calories 588, fat 17.2 g, carbs 42 g,
Protein 19.5 g, sodium 1847 mg

# Classic Pork Stir Fry

*Serves: 2 - Prep. time: 2–3 minutes, plus marinating time – Cooking time: 6–8 minutes*

**Ingredients:**
1 teaspoon olive oil
½ pound pork loin, cubed
1 cup green peppers, diced
1 medium tomato, sliced
1 teaspoon ground black pepper
For serving: chopped greens
Steamed rice (optional)

Marinade:
3 tablespoons fish sauce
1 clove garlic, diced
¼ cup red wine
2 teaspoons sesame oil
1 teaspoon grated ginger
1 teaspoon chili flakes

**Preparation:**
1. Combine the marinade ingredients in a bowl.
2. Place the marinade and meat in a resealable bag. Shake well and marinate for 1–2 hours.
3. In a skillet, heat the olive oil over medium.
4. Cook the pork for 3–5 minutes, reserving the marinade.
5. Add the green pepper, tomato, and black pepper, and stir fry for 2 minutes.
6. Add the marinade liquid to the skillet, bring it to a boil, and cook for 1 minute.
7. Serve with chopped greens and/or steamed rice.

**Nutrition facts per serving**
Calories 623, fat 18 g, carbs 49.2 g,
Protein 18.4 g, sodium 1841 mg

# Vegetarian/Vegan Recipes

## Arugula Pecan Pear Salad

*Serves: 2 - Prep. time: 5 minutes - Cooking time: 6 minutes*

**Ingredients:**
¼ cup chopped pecans
10 ounces arugula
2 pears, thinly sliced
2 tablespoons champagne vinegar
2 tablespoons olive oil
1 tablespoon shallot, finely minced
¼ teaspoon sea salt
¼ teaspoon black pepper, ground
¼ teaspoon Dijon mustard

**Preparation:**
1. Preheat the oven to 350°F.
2. Arrange the pecans on a baking sheet. Toast until fragrant, about 5–6 minutes.
3. Remove them from the oven and let them cool down.
4. In a mixing bowl, mix the pecans, arugula, and pears.
5. In a small bowl, whisk together the vinegar, olive oil, shallot, salt, pepper, and mustard.
6. Toss with the salad and serve.

**Nutrition facts per serving**
Calories 462, fat 16 g, carbs 52.2 g,
Protein 10.7 g, sodium 190 mg

# Tomato Veggie Lentils

*Serves: 2 - Prep. time: 2–3 min - Cooking time: 12–15 min*

**Ingredients:**
1 tablespoon olive oil
1 carrot, diced
1 celery stalk, diced
1 small onion, diced
1 clove garlic, minced
1 (15 ounce) can lentils, drained and rinsed
1 cup tomatoes, chopped
1 teaspoon curry powder
Salt and pepper to taste
1 tablespoon cilantro, chopped

**Preparation:**
1. In a saucepan, heat the olive oil over medium-high heat. Add the carrot, celery, and onion.
2. Continue cooking until the vegetables soften, about 4–5 minutes.
3. Add the garlic and cook until it is fragrant, about 30 seconds.
4. Add the lentils, tomatoes, and curry powder; cook for 6–8 minutes.
5. Season with salt and pepper.
6. Stir in the cilantro, and serve.

**Nutrition facts per serving**
Calories 325, fat 8.6 g, carbs 41.3 g,
Protein 18 g, sodium 31 mg

# Pomegranate Green Salad

*Serves: 2 - Prep. time: 5 minutes - Cooking time: 0 minutes*

**Ingredients:**
10 ounces baby spinach
1 pomegranate, pips only
1 cup fresh blackberries
¼ red onion, thinly sliced
½ cup chopped pecans
3 tablespoons extra-virgin olive oil
1 tablespoon balsamic vinegar
Salt and pepper to taste

**Preparation:**
1. In a mixing bowl, combine the spinach, pomegranate pips, blackberries, red onion, and pecans.
2. In another bowl, whisk together the olive oil, vinegar, salt, and pepper.
3. Toss with the salad and serve.

**Nutrition facts per serving**
Calories 712, fat 39 g, carbs 26.8 g,
Protein 6.8 g, sodium 361 mg

# Tangy Chickpea Spinach

*Serves: 2 - Prep. time: 2–3 minutes - Cooking time: 10 minutes*

**Ingredients:**
3 tablespoons olive oil
1 (15-ounce) can chickpeas, drained and rinsed
10 ounces baby spinach
½ teaspoon sea salt
Ground black pepper to taste
Juice and zest of 1 lemon

**Preparation:**
1. In a large skillet, heat the olive oil over medium-high heat.
2. Add the chickpeas and cook for 4–5 minutes.
3. Add the spinach and stir; cook for 2–3 more minutes.
4. Add the salt and pepper, lemon juice, and lemon zest. Combine well and serve warm.

**Nutrition facts per serving**
Calories 572, fat 16.2 g, carbs 18 g,
Protein 21.6 g, sodium 297 mg

# Mushroom Onion Curry

*Serves: 2 - Prep. time: 2–3 min - Cooking time: 13-14 min*

### Ingredients:
1 teaspoon coconut oil
1 small onion, thinly sliced
1 small carrot, peeled and julienned
¼ cup shiitake mushrooms, sliced
2 cloves garlic, minced
1 cup coconut milk
1 teaspoon lime juice
½ cup vegetable stock
¼ teaspoon sea salt
1 teaspoon curry powder

### Preparation:
1. In a large saucepan, heat the coconut oil over medium-high heat.
2. Add the onion, carrot, and mushrooms, and cook for about 6 minutes, until they begin to soften.
3. Stir in the garlic and cook until fragrant, about 30 seconds.
4. Add the coconut milk, lime juice, vegetable stock, lime juice, salt, and curry powder.
5. Boil the mixture for 2–4 minutes and serve warm.

### Nutrition facts per serving
Calories 571, fat 34.6 g, carbs 24.1 g,
Protein 2.4 g, sodium 311 mg

# Chili Mixed Bean Stew

*Serves: 2 - Prep. time: 2–3 minutes - Cooking time: 13 minutes*

**Ingredients:**
1 tablespoon olive oil
½ onion, diced
2 cloves garlic, minced
1 cup kidney beans, drained and rinsed
1 cup black beans, drained and rinsed
1 cup pinto beans, drained and rinsed
1 (15 ounce) can roasted tomatoes with peppers
1 ½ tablespoons chili powder
1 cup vegetable stock
½ teaspoon sea salt

**Preparation:**
1. In a large saucepan, heat the olive oil over medium-high heat.
2. Add the onion. Cook until it begins to soften, 2–3 minutes.
3. Add the garlic and cook until fragrant, about 30 seconds.
4. Add the beans, tomatoes, chili powder, vegetable stock, and salt.
5. Simmer for 10 minutes, and serve.

**Nutrition facts per serving**
Calories 586, fat 18.7 g, carbs 52 g,
Protein 31.4 g, sodium 892 mg

# Tangy Tofu

*Serves: 2 - Prep. time: 2–3 minutes - Cooking time: 8 minutes*

## Ingredients:
¼ cup orange juice
½ tablespoon unseasoned rice vinegar
2 tablespoons soy sauce
½ teaspoon ginger, grated
½ teaspoon cornstarch
1 tablespoon olive oil
2 cloves garlic, minced
½ pound extra-firm tofu, drained, cut in 1-inch cubes

## Preparation:
1. In a mixing bowl, whisk together the orange juice, vinegar, soy sauce, ginger, and cornstarch. Set aside.
2. In a medium saucepan, heat the olive oil on medium.
3. Add the garlic and cook until fragrant, about 30 seconds.
4. Add the tofu and cook for 3–4 minutes, until lightly browned.
5. Add the orange sauce to the pan.
6. Simmer until the sauce thickens, 3–4 minutes. Serve warm.

## Nutrition facts per serving
Calories 194, fat 12 g, carbs 8.6 g,
Protein 11.4 g, sodium 924 mg

# Peanut Butter Noodles

*Serves: 2 - Prep. time: 2–3 minutes - Cooking time: 10 minutes*

**Ingredients:**
½ package soba noodles
¼ cup vegetable stock
½ tablespoon ginger, minced
1 clove garlic, minced
2 tablespoons soy sauce
2 tablespoons peanut butter
½ teaspoon chili paste
2 green onions (white and green parts), chopped
Chopped peanuts

**Preparation:**
1. Cook the noodles in salted water for 7–8 minutes. Drain the water and set the noodles aside.
2. Meanwhile, in a small saucepan, combine the vegetable stock, ginger, garlic, soy sauce, peanut butter, and chili paste.
3. Heat the sauce on medium high until hot, 3–4 minutes.
4. Mix the sauce with the noodles and serve topped with green onions and peanuts.

**Nutrition facts per serving**
Calories 142, fat 8.2 g, carbs 12.8 g,
Protein 5.7 g, sodium 854 mg

# Mushroom Tofu Dinner

*Serves: 2 - Prep. time: 2–3 minutes - Cooking time: 10 minutes*

**Ingredients:**
2 cloves garlic, minced
½ tablespoon fresh ginger, grated
¼ cup soy sauce
¼ teaspoon chili oil
½ tablespoon sesame oil
½ pound extra-firm tofu, cut in bite-sized pieces
8 ounces shiitake mushrooms, chopped
2 green onions, sliced (white and green parts)
2 tablespoons cilantro, chopped
1 tablespoon sesame seeds

**Preparation:**
1. Heat your broiler to high.
2. In a mixing bowl, combine the garlic, ginger, soy sauce, chili oil, and sesame oil.
3. Arrange the tofu and mushrooms in a baking dish, and pour the sauce mixture over the top.
4. Cook under the boiler until the sauce bubbles, 8–10 minutes.
5. Top with the green onions, cilantro, and sesame seeds. Serve warm.

**Nutrition facts per serving**
Calories 257, fat 11.2 g, carbs 21.7 g,
Protein 14 g, sodium 1176 mg

# Desserts

## Chilled Choco Pudding

*Serves: 2 - Prep. time: 2–3 minutes –
Cooking time: 10–12 minutes (plus cooling time)*

### Ingredients:
3 tablespoons sugar
3 tablespoons unsweetened cocoa powder
1 ½ cups unsweetened almond milk, divided
2 tablespoons cornstarch
Pinch of sea salt
½ teaspoon vanilla extract

### Preparation:
1. In a large saucepan, combine the sugar and cocoa powder.
2. Add 1 cup of almond milk, and stir to combine.
3. Heat over medium-high until it comes to a boil, and remove it from the heat.
4. In another bowl, whisk the remaining milk and cornstarch together.
5. Gradually add the cornstarch slurry to the hot cocoa mixture, whisking constantly.
6. Boil for 1–2 minutes, to thicken.
7. Stir in the vanilla, and let the pudding cool completely before serving, 30–60 minutes.

### Nutrition facts per serving
Calories 132, fat 2.8 g, carbs 26.2 g,
Protein 1.7 g, sodium 192 mg

# Pecan Apple Compote Delight

*Serves: 2 - Prep. time: 2–3 minutes - Cooking time: 13 minutes*

## Ingredients:
2 sweet-tart apples, cored and peeled
¼ cup apple juice
Juice of half a lemon
2 tablespoons brown sugar
⅛ teaspoon grated nutmeg
½ teaspoon ground cinnamon
Pinch of sea salt
2 tablespoons chopped pecans

## Preparation:
1. In a saucepan, combine the apples, apple juice, lemon juice, brown sugar, nutmeg, cinnamon, and salt over medium-high heat. Cook for 8–10 minutes, stirring often.
2. Remove the saucepan from the heat and set it aside to cool.
3. Meanwhile, in a dry skillet, toast the pecans, stirring frequently, for 2–3 minutes.
4. Serve the dessert with toasted pecans on top.

## Nutrition facts per serving
Calories 247, fat 5.3 g, carbs 28.6 g,
Protein 1.8 g, sodium 64 mg

# Dessert Date Truffles

*Serves: Makes around 12 truffles - Prep. time: 10 minutes – Cooking time: 0 minutes*

**Ingredients:**
½ cup sweetened cocoa powder
¼ cup maple syrup
½ cup unsweetened shredded coconut
1 cup dates, pitted
1 cup almonds
1 teaspoon vanilla extract
1 teaspoon almond extract
¼ teaspoon sea salt

**Preparation:**
1. In a food processor or blender, combine all the ingredients and process until smooth. Chill the mixture for about 1 hour.
2. Roll the mixture to make small balls.
3. One by one, roll the balls in cocoa powder to coat evenly.
4. Serve immediately, or refrigerate and serve chilled.

**Nutrition facts per serving**
Calories 492, fat 24 g, carbs 36.4 g,
Protein 11.7 g, sodium 153 mg

# Pineapple Rum Delight

*Serves: 2 - Prep. time: 2-3 minutes - Cooking time: 10 minutes*

**Ingredients:**
1 tablespoon butter
1 ½ tablespoons brown sugar
1 ½ tablespoons rum
1 small pineapple, peeled and cut in ½-inch rounds
1 tablespoon lemon juice

**Preparation:**
1. Melt the butter in a skillet, and add the sugar. Stir until dissolved, and then add the pineapple. Combine gently.
2. Cook on medium-high heat until the pineapple begins to caramelize, 4–5 minutes.
3. Add the rum, and cook for 4 more minutes.
4. Mix in the lemon juice, and serve warm!

**Nutrition facts per serving**
Calories 263, fat 6 g, carbs 22.6 g,
Protein 0.8 g, sodium 42 mg

# Creamy Fruity Frozen Mousse

*Serves: 2 - Prep. time: 5 minutes - Cooking time: 0 minutes*

**Ingredients:**
½ cup mango chunks, frozen
½ cup raspberries, frozen
½ cup pineapple chunks, frozen
3 ounces sweetened condensed milk, chilled
½ cup whipped cream
Chopped strawberries, walnuts, and almonds to garnish

**Preparation:**
1. Blend all the ingredients in a blender EXCEPT the strawberries, walnuts, and almonds, until smooth.
2. Spoon the mousse into serving glasses.
3. Top with strawberries, crushed walnuts, and almonds.

**Nutrition facts per serving**
Calories 323, fat 14 g, carbs 39.2 g,
Protein 7.5 g, sodium 253 mg

# Recipe Index

Breakfast Recipes _____ 3
   Spiced Orange Couscous _____ 3
   Cinnamon Apple Classic Oatmeal _____ 4
   Flax Almond Crepes _____ 5
   Berry Breakfast Granola _____ 6
   Nutty Peach Breakfast Bowl _____ 7
Chicken & Poultry Recipes _____ 9
   Spiced Pepper Turkey _____ 9
   Barbecue Orange Chicken _____ 10
   Chicken Lettuce Cups _____ 11
   Lemongrass Pasta Chicken _____ 12
   Spiced Turkey Burger Patties _____ 13
   Fried Asparagus Chicken _____ 14
   Classic Honey Chicken _____ 15
   Mayo Grilled Chicken _____ 16
Beef Recipes _____ 17
   Bacon Veggie Steak _____ 17
   Barbecued Mirin Short Ribs _____ 18
   Garlic Steak with Greens _____ 19
   Broccoli Garlic Steak _____ 20
   Jalapeño Sweet Beef _____ 21
   Bean Sprout Beef Salad _____ 22
   Beef Burger Patties _____ 23
   Berry Sauce Beef _____ 24
Fish & Seafood Recipes _____ 25
   Sardine Arugula Salad _____ 25
   Tuna Pineapple Treat _____ 26
   Shrimp Potato Salad _____ 27
   Whitefish and Veggies _____ 28
   Tuna Lettuce Pasta Time _____ 29
   Wine and Tomato Mussels _____ 30
   Buttery White Wine Prawns _____ 31

Pork & Lamb Recipes _____33
  Grilled Pork Mango Meal _____33
  Ham and Bacon Melt _____34
  Spiced Lamb Sausages _____35
  Sweet Tarragon Lamb _____36
  Spiced Pita Lamb Burgers _____37
  Peas and Lemongrass Pork _____38
  Mushroom Basil Pork Fry _____39
  Classic Pork Stir Fry _____41
Vegetarian/Vegan Recipes _____43
  Arugula Pecan Pear Salad _____43
  Tomato Veggie Lentils _____44
  Pomegranate Green Salad _____45
  Tangy Chickpea Spinach _____46
  Mushroom Onion Curry _____47
  Chili Mixed Bean Stew _____48
  Tangy Tofu _____49
  Peanut Butter Noodles _____50
  Mushroom Tofu Dinner _____51
Desserts _____53
  Chilled Choco Pudding _____53
  Pecan Apple Compote Delight _____54
  Dessert Date Truffles _____55
  Pineapple Rum Delight _____56
  Creamy Fruity Frozen Mousse _____57

# Also by Louise Davidson

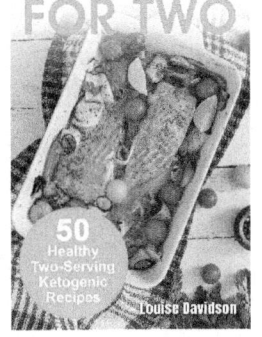

- Slow Cooking for Two: 100 Healthy Two-Serving Slow Cooker Recipes
- Cast Iron for Two: 50 Healthy Two-Serving Cast Iron Recipes
- Ketogenic for Two: 50 Healthy Two-Serving Ketogenic Recipes
- 5-Ingredient Slow Cooking for Two: 50 Healthy Two-Serving 5-Ingredient Slow Cooker Recipes
- Air Fryer for Two: 50 Healthy Two-Serving Air Fryer Recipes
- Desserts for Two: 50 Easy-to-Make Two-Serving Dessert Recipes
- Instant Pot for Two: 50 Healthy Two-Serving Pressure Cooker Recipes
- Dutch Oven Cooking: Easy One-Pot Meal Recipes
- Home Canning and Preserving: Recipes for Beginners

# Appendix
# Cooking Conversion Charts

## 1. Measuring Equivalent Chart

| Type | Imperial | Imperial | Metric |
|---|---|---|---|
| Weight | 1 dry ounce | | 28g |
| | 1 pound | 16 dry ounces | 0.45 kg |
| Volume | 1 teaspoon | | 5 ml |
| | 1 dessert spoon | 2 teaspoons | 10 ml |
| | 1 tablespoon | 3 teaspoons | 15 ml |
| | 1 Australian tablespoon | 4 teaspoons | 20 ml |
| | 1 fluid ounce | 2 tablespoons | 30 ml |
| | 1 cup | 16 tablespoons | 240 ml |
| | 1 cup | 8 fluid ounces | 240 ml |
| | 1 pint | 2 cups | 470 ml |
| | 1 quart | 2 pints | 0.95 l |
| | 1 gallon | 4 quarts | 3.8 l |
| Length | 1 inch | | 2.54 cm |

\* Numbers are rounded to the closest equivalent

## 2. Oven Temperature Equivalent Chart

| Fahrenheit (°F) | Celsius (°C) | Gas Mark |
|---|---|---|
| 220 | 100 | |
| 225 | 110 | 1/4 |
| 250 | 120 | 1/2 |
| 275 | 140 | 1 |
| 300 | 150 | 2 |
| 325 | 160 | 3 |
| 350 | 180 | 4 |
| 375 | 190 | 5 |
| 400 | 200 | 6 |
| 425 | 220 | 7 |
| 450 | 230 | 8 |
| 475 | 250 | 9 |
| 500 | 260 | |

\* Celsius (°C) = T (°F)-32] * 5/9
\*\* Fahrenheit (°F) = T (°C) * 9/5 + 32
\*\*\* Numbers are rounded to the closest equivalent

Printed in Great Britain
by Amazon